NORTH AMERICAN MYTHS & LEGENDS

AS TOLD BY PHILIP ARDAGH

ILLUSTRATED BY OLIVIA RAYNER

Belitha Press

MYTH OR LEGEND?

Long before people could read or write, stories were passed on by word of mouth. Every time they were told, they changed a little, with a new character added here and a twist to the plot there. From these ever-changing tales, myths and legends were born.

WHAT IS A MYTH?

A myth is a traditional story that isn't based on something that really happened and is usually about superhuman beings. Myths are made up, but they help to explain local customs or natural phenomena. Many North American myths include gods who can turn themselves into animals.

WHAT IS A LEGEND?

A legend is very like a myth. The difference is that a legend might be based on an event that really happened, or a person who really existed. That's not to say that the story hasn't changed over the years.

NORTH AMERICAN PEOPLES

The myths and legends in this book come from three very different North American peoples: Native North Americans, European settlers and African-Americans.

NATIVE NORTH AMERICANS

Native North Americans, who were called 'Indians' by the Europeans, were the first people to live in North America. They walked from Asia about 15,000 years ago when the two continents were linked by ice. They formed many different tribes. You can find out more about these tribes on pages 4 and 5.

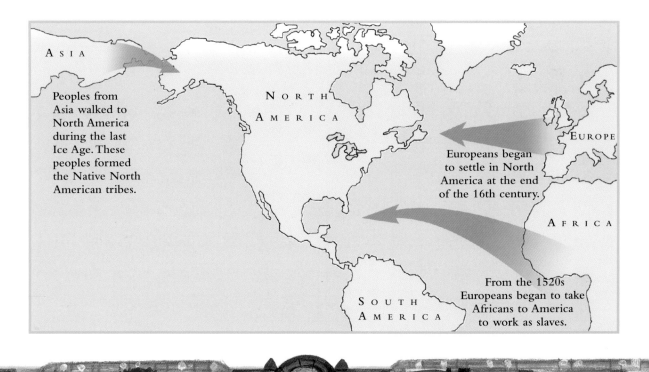

ASIA

Peoples from Asia walked to North America during the last Ice Age. These peoples formed the Native North American tribes.

NORTH AMERICA

EUROPE

Europeans began to settle in North America at the end of the 16th century.

AFRICA

SOUTH AMERICA

From the 1520s Europeans began to take Africans to America to work as slaves.

EUROPEAN SETTLERS

The Vikings arrived in North America about 1,000 years ago, but the first Europeans to stay and build their homes there arrived about 100 years after Christopher Columbus discovered the Bahamas in 1492. Most of these early settlers lived on the east coast. It was not until the 19th century that people began to move west and to settle in the rest of North America.

AFRICAN-AMERICANS

African-Americans were originally brought to North America by the Europeans to work as slaves on cotton plantations. This terrible trade in humans continued until 1865 when slavery was finally abolished.

LIVING MYTHS AND LEGENDS

Native American myths and legends are very much alive and are still told today. They are an important part of the cultures of the various tribes and are used in art and religious ceremonies. It is important to remember that what one person might see as a myth or legend, another might see as a part of his or her religion.

HOW DO WE KNOW?

In the 18th and 19th centuries, a number of Europeans visited the Native North American tribes and recorded their way of life, including their myths and legends. The stories retold in this book are based on some of these early written accounts.

LATER MYTHS AND LEGENDS

The European and African-American stories are far more recent. Most were told by the 19th-century European settlers and their African slaves. Like the Native American myths and legends before them, these tales were originally passed on by word of mouth and were only later written down. And they are still changing as they are retold today. Many African-American stories – first told in North America by slaves – have their roots in African myths and legends, but were adapted to fit this new life far away from home.

NOTE FROM THE AUTHOR

Myths and legends from different cultures were told in very different ways. The purpose of this book is to tell *versions* of these stories, but not to try to copy the way in which they were actually told. I hope that you enjoy them and that this book will make you want to find out more about the lives of the different North American peoples, as well as their myths and legends.

NATIVE NORTH AMERICANS

Native North American tribes were scattered right across North America – from the Canadian Inuit in the north to the Calusans in what is now southern Florida. The term Native North Americans includes many different peoples with different beliefs and ideas. Some tribes are grouped together by a shared language, such as the Algonquian-speaking peoples who are made up of over ten tribes.

SHARED BELIEFS

Native North American tribes share many beliefs, even though their ways of life and their myths and legends may be different. A common belief is that everything on Earth is somehow connected – every plant, every animal, every person, every speck of dirt or drop of water. Harming something for no good reason will upset the balance of nature and will, in the end, harm everything else.

SHARED MYTHS

Both the Cherokees and the Creeks have a myth which tells how bears were once a human tribe. According to this myth, when food became scarce, the bears went into the forest and returned as 'hairy humans'. They offered to be hunted by the others for their meat and skins. This was their sacrifice so that the others could survive. This is also why the Cherokees and Creeks say that you must always respect what you hunt.

COMMON THEMES

There are other common themes in Native North American myths and legends. Many myths about the creation of the Earth include a flood, and a number of different tribes have stories about a coyote and a hare as mischievous trickster gods. The shaman – part doctor and part priest – is an important member of some Native American communities and appears in many tribes' myths and legends.

LOST HOMELANDS

Over time, as their land has been populated by settlers from overseas, many Native North Americans have lost their traditional homelands. Large numbers were resettled on reservations, but still have strong ties with their land. Between the arrival of European settlers in the late 1500s and 1900, the Native North American population dropped from about one million to a few hundred thousand.

This map shows the 'culture areas' of the many Native North American tribes. Each culture area, representing a number of tribes with a similar way of life, is shown in a different colour.

ARCTIC

SUBARCTIC

NORTHWEST COAST

PLATEAU

GREAT BASIN

CALIFORNIA

PLAINS

NORTHEAST

SOUTHEAST

SOUTHWEST

KEY TO THE TRIBES

Arctic tribes include:
Inuit (Eskimo), Netsilik and Aleut

Subarctic tribes include:
Cree, Naskapi, Ingalik and Beaver

Northwest Coast tribes include:
Chinook, Haida and Nootka

Plateau tribes include:
Shuswap, Nez Perce and Yakima

Plains tribes include:
Sioux, Comanche, Blackfoot, Cheyenne, Crow and Pawnee

Northeast tribes include:
Algonquian, Iroquois, Chippewa, Mahican, Micmac and Shawnee

Great Basin tribes include:
Ute, Paiute and Kawaiisu

California tribes include:
Maidu, Hupa and Monache

Southwest tribes include:
Navajo, Apache, Pueblo and Hopi

Southeast tribes include:
Creek, Cherokee, Caddo, Apalachee, Calusan and Chickasaw

TALES OF THE GREAT HARE

According to tales told by the Algonquian-speaking tribes, Michabo the god was a son of the West Wind and a bringer of light. Mighty in word and deed, he took the form of the rabbit's cousin, the hare.

Michabo, the Great Hare, was swimming in the ocean. With his powerful hind legs, he was an excellent swimmer. He dived deep down to where the sea was darkest blue, with his long ears streaming out behind him.

He had never swum so deep before, and he decided to see if he could reach the very bottom. On he went, deeper and deeper, until his lungs seemed fit to burst. Then he touched the ocean floor.

In triumph, he plucked up a single grain of sand and swam back to the surface, clutching it in his paw. He then placed the trophy of his successful dive on the ocean surface. There it turned from a single grain into a thousand grains, and from a thousand into a million... until it grew into an island, then a continent, then larger still.

But how big was it? The Algonquian tell how one day a wolf cub found itself on the edge of the land and decided to trek across it. By the time the wolf was fully-grown, the other side was still too far ahead to see... but on he went, determined to reach the edge. For years and years he wandered, until, finally, his years ran out – he had reached old age and still hadn't completed his journey. When the animal lay down to die after a long life, the end of the land was still nowhere in sight. *That's* how big the land was.

Many peoples – of many tribes and many races – came to live on this land. This piece of land, created from a single grain of sand, is what we now think of as Earth, and Michabo the Great Hare was its creator.

One day, Great Hare was walking past a mighty river which flowed between the trees like a giant, silver snake. A boy stood in the shallows of the crystal-clear water, as still as the stones on the rocky river bed. Suddenly, there was a flash of silvery light beneath the surface as a fish darted by. The boy hurled a spear at it – the sharp point only narrowly missing its target. The boy picked up the spear and became still once more, to wait for the next fish to swim by.

Great Hare lay down against a rock in the afternoon sunshine and thought about what he had just seen. He knew that by the time the boy had grown into a young man, he would probably be a fine hunter and would catch many fish with his spear for his wife and children. But surely there was an easier way to catch food?

Still thinking about this problem, Great Hare drifted off to sleep in the lazy afternoon sun. When he awoke, he felt a tingling on the top of his head. Imagine his surprise when he found that, while he'd been sleeping, a spider had spun her delicate web between his ears!

But Great Hare was not angry. He laughed. He carefully caught the spider between his paws and gently placed her on a rock, where she scuttled for cover... but not before he had studied the delicate web she'd spun. It had given the god an idea.

The spider used her web to catch flies... flies she would later eat. She would spin her web on a branch – or even between the ears of a god – and wait for the flies to fly into it and become trapped.

Why not make a similar web from twine? It would have to be much bigger and stronger than the spider's web, but the idea was the same. Instead of casting a web into the air to catch flies, people could cast a net into the water to catch fish. And that is how the fishing net was invented – thanks to Great Hare and a spider.

On another occasion, Michabo the Great Hare had left his home in the east – the place of light and good – and was sitting by another river bank, drawing patterns in the wet sand with a twig. A man and woman passed by, greeted him, then went into the forest to pick herbs.

Without much thought, Great Hare lazily drew simple outline pictures of them.

On their return, they passed the Great Hare once more and the woman glanced down at the images he'd drawn in the sand. She asked him what he was doing.

'Drawing pictures,' he told them.

The man laughed. 'That looks like the two of us walking side-by-side,' he said with glee and pointed at the pictures in the sand.

'And those trees look like the forest over there,' said the woman excitedly. 'You are clever! It's like a story – not in words but in squiggles in the sand. Anyone who sees them will know a man and woman went into the forest.'

'And came back with herbs,' said the Great Hare, drawing another picture in the row. He leapt up in delight, and sniffed the wind with his twitching nose, just as any ordinary hare does when it has a great idea.

'If I were to draw several pictures, each with a different meaning, then people could leave each other messages,' he said gleefully. 'They wouldn't even have to be in the same place at the same time to speak to each other. What a thoroughly useful invention!'

And that is how the Algonquian say that picture writing was invented.

Time and time again, Michabo proved himself a true friend to the people. He taught them many tricks in hunting – such as when to wait and when to pounce, and ways to track prey downwind so that it won't catch your scent in the air – and he gave them many lucky charms to help them. But, before each winter came, he would leave his human friends behind and go home for his long sleep, ready to return the next spring.

Creator, inventor, trickster or fool, there was always a place in the Great Hare's heart for his people, and in the hearts of the Algonquian for him.

THE QUEST
FOR HEALING

Nekumonta, the Iroquois brave, never killed an animal for sport and loved the plants and trees around him. When a terrible plague descended on his village, his kindness to nature was repaid.

Winter had come to Nekumonta's village and the snow was thick on the ground. But something worse than snow had come to visit the village that year – a dreadful plague. No one seemed safe – men, women and children had all died from it. Those who hadn't yet caught the plague were exhausted from looking after the ill and sending off the dead.

Never had there been such sadness in the village. Husbands lost wives. Mothers lost children. Brothers lost sisters. Whole families were wiped out. Along with the snow came the plague... and along with the plague came sadness and despair.

Nekumonta had lost all his family to this terrible disease – all, that is, except for his beautiful wife, Shanewis. But now she had caught the disease and her days amongst the living were numbered. She called for Nekumonta and insisted that he carry her outside.

When he protested, she said: 'Husband, we both know that death will come whether I stay in the warmth or sit beneath the sky, where I can hear the spirits of my dead loved ones call my name. Please, please, do as I ask.'

So Nekumonta wrapped his beloved wife in extra blankets and carried her into the open, laying her down in a place cleared of snow. Sure enough, the grey skies were filled with the spirits of those who had departed this life, and they called down to Shanewis.

'Join us,' they cried out. 'Be free from the pain and suffering brought by the plague.'

But Nekumonta would have none of it.

'Pay no heed to their calls until I return from my quest,' he begged his dying wife. 'Then decide if you have no choice but to join them.'

'What quest?' asked Shanewis, her forehead beaded with sweat.

'We know that the Manitou has planted healing herbs,' he said. 'I will find them and bring them back to you and our people.'

'I will wait, husband,' said Shanewis, 'because if anyone can succeed, it will be you.'

For many tribes, Manitou means the spirit inside everything – from rocks and plants to humans. For the Iroquois, the Manitou is the name given to the greatest and most powerful of all their gods. His healing herbs would cure Shanewis… if only her husband could find them.

With his wife back in the warmth of their home, Nekumonta set off on his quest for the healing herbs.

This would have been a difficult task at the best of times, but it was made even harder by the snow which covered much of the ground. Nekumonta had to dig in the snow to try and find the herbs and he didn't even know where they were planted. Using his knowledge of nature, he could only guess at where they were likely to grow.

At the end of the first day, a rabbit bounced past Nekumonta as he was kneeling in the snow, digging away with his hands.

'Do you know where the Manitou has planted the herbs that will help cure my people?' Nekumonta asked, but the rabbit didn't know and continued on its way, leaving behind its tracks in the snow.

Later, as darkness drew in at the end of the short winter's day, the Iroquois brave caught sight of a grizzly bear watching him from the depths of the forest. Nekumonta asked the bear about the healing herbs, but the bear knew nothing, and lumbered off between the trees.

The next afternoon, having travelled far and wide, Nekumonta saw a doe – a female deer – chewing at the shoots of a plant sticking out of the snow. The doe recognized him and, knowing that he was a friend to the animals and meant her no harm, she did not run and hide.

Nekumonta patted her gently and said: 'Everyone in my village is dying and my beautiful wife, Shanewis, is amongst them. If you know where the Manitou has planted the healing herbs, please lead me to them. They are our only hope.'

But the doe didn't know where the Manitou had planted the herbs, so she twitched her ears and disappeared into the forest. The story was the same with every animal he met after that. None of them could help him.

On the third night, Nekumonta was near to giving up. Weak and exhausted, he wrapped himself in his blanket and fell asleep.

While he slept, the animals of the forest held a meeting.

'Nekumonta is a good human,' said the grizzly bear. 'He only kills when he has to, as is the way with us animals.'

'And he treats our homes with respect too,' said the rabbit. 'He cares about the trees and plants around him.'

'Do you think we should help him?' asked the doe.

'Yes,' said the rabbit. 'But how can we?'

'Perhaps we could call to the great Manitou for his help?' suggested the grizzly bear. 'Then he will realize that all living things want Nekumonta to succeed in his quest.'

So the rabbit, the grizzly bear, the doe and all the other animals stood in a clearing in the forest and cried out to the Manitou to save Shanewis from the plague. The Manitou heard their cries and, touched by the animals' loyalty to a human, decided to help Nekumonta.

That night, Shanewis came to Nekumonta in a dream – pale-faced and very thin. She began to sing him a strange and beautiful song, but he could not understand the words and they soon turned into the music of a waterfall.

When he awoke, the music of the waterfall was still there with its sparkling chorus of voices – as pure and crystal-clear as spring water.

It said: 'Find us... Free us... Then Shanewis and your people shall be saved.'

But despite the beautiful music, there was no waterfall – not even a tiny stream – to be seen.

'Who are you?' called Nekumonta.

'We are the Healing Waters,' said the chorus. 'Free us.'

'Where are you?' cried Nekumonta in despair, for the chorus of sparkling voices sounded so near, yet he could not find it.

'Free us,' sang the chorus once more.

With a new lease of life, Nekumonta hunted high and low, but he couldn't find the Healing Waters anywhere... even though the voice of the chorus remained strong. Then he realized why. The Healing Waters were flowing directly beneath his feet. They were an underground spring!

Watched by the animals of the forest, Nekumonta first scraped away the snow, then hacked away at the hard soil with a flint, until a jet of water spurted high into the air and began flowing down the hillside. He had found the Healing Waters!

Exhausted, Nekumonta stepped into the path of the ice-cold waters and bathed himself in them. Their magical powers gave him strength, and all his tiredness was suddenly gone. Now he felt fitter and stronger than he had ever done before.

He filled a skin bottle with the Healing Waters and ran down the hillside to the village. The other villagers rushed out of their homes to greet him.

'We are saved!' he cried. 'We are saved!'

Soon everyone from the village had drunk and bathed in the waters and were well again. They thanked Nekumonta with all their hearts. He had succeeded in his quest and the plague had been defeated.

When Nekumonta learned of the part the animals had played in helping him to save Shanewis and the village, he gave them thanks. In turn, the animals gave thanks to the great Manitou who is, after all, master of everything. Nekumonta and Shanewis lived for many summers and had many children.

THE CRYING THAT DEFEATED A GOD

To the Algonquian-speaking tribes, Glooskap was a great god and trickster. He was afraid of no one, and believed that there was nothing and nobody he could not conquer.

Glooskap had been away from his people for a long time. He had been away facing his enemies and had defeated them all through his bravery, cunning and quick wit.

When he returned to one of his tribes, Glooskap boasted about just how great he was. 'There's no one left in this world who doesn't fear me or won't obey me,' he said.

'Are you sure about that, master?' asked a woman. 'I know of one who will not obey you.'

Surprised at the news, but thrilled by the challenge, Glooskap demanded to know the name of this being.

'He is called Wasis,' said the woman.

'And he does not fear me?' asked Glooskap.

'No,' said the woman. 'He always does exactly what he wants. He will not obey even you, master.'

'Then this Wasis must be a very mighty one,' said Glooskap.

'In his way,' agreed the woman.

'Is he as tall as the Kewawkqu'?' Glooskap demanded. The Kewawkqu' were a race of giants and magicians.

'No,' said the woman. 'He is smaller than a goblin.'

'Is his magic greater than the Medecolin?' Glooskap demanded. The Medecolin were cunning sorcerers.

'No,' said the woman. 'He knows no magic.'

'Is he as wicked as Pamola?' Glooskap demanded. Pamola was an evil spirit of the night.

'No,' said the woman. 'Wasis is none of these things. He is not a giant. He is not a sorcerer and there is no wickedness in him at all.'

'Yet he does not fear me and he will not obey me!' boomed Glooskap, who was most puzzled by the thought of the mighty Wasis. 'Will you take me to him?'

'If you wish it, master,' said the woman. 'Wasis lives close by. Come.'

With that, she led Glooskap to an ordinary wigwam. The dome-shaped house was made from a wooden frame covered with pieces of birch bark sewn together.

'Wasis lives here in the village?' asked Glooskap, shocked at the very suggestion. Why had he never heard of him? And why didn't someone as mighty as he live in one of the grander wigwams, with animal skins instead of bark for walls?

'Yes,' said the woman. 'This is his home.'

They entered the wigwam and the god looked around. It seemed familiar. 'Isn't this your home?' he asked.

The woman nodded her head. 'Yes, master, but now it is Wasis' home too.'

'Where is he, then?' asked Glooskap.

The woman pointed to a baby who was sitting on a rug, sucking a piece of maple sugar. 'That is Wasis,' she said.

'But he is no more than a baby!' Glooskap said, laughing loudly.

'No more and no less, master,' the woman agreed. 'He is my son.' She knew that Glooskap was always away having adventures and had never had to look after a child in his whole life. He didn't know how different young children were from other human beings!

Glooskap decided to use his charm to make Wasis obey him. He smiled at the baby. 'Come here, Wasis,' he said.

Wasis smiled back, but didn't move. He just sat in the middle of the rug, gurgling happily to himself.

Then Glooskap put his hands to his mouth and made the sound of birdsong.

It was beautiful music, and Wasis' mother was enchanted by the sound. But it was not intended for her. It was intended to attract the attention of Wasis, and he wasn't in the least bit interested. He showed far more interest in the piece of maple sugar he was sucking.

Furious that anyone dared ignore him – a mighty god – Glooskap exploded in a terrible rage. 'Come here at once!' he shouted at Wasis, but still this had no effect.

Upset by this stranger who had come into his home and was now shouting and waving his arms around, Wasis refused to obey the god. He burst into tears. The louder Glooskap's rage became, the louder Wasis howled… and still he would not move from his spot on the rug.

Finally, Glooskap turned to magic. He began to sing a song so powerful that it was enough to wake the dead. Some say that it was a song so woven with magic that it made all the evil spirits scurry to the deepest depths of Mother Earth to escape from it.

Wasis stopped howling and seemed soothed by the tune. But soon he was bored by it – he yawned loudly and his eyelids began to droop.

Utterly defeated, Glooskap fled the wigwam, shaking with anger. The woman scooped up Wasis in her arms and held him close to her. She walked out through the doorway and watched the enraged god stomping off through the camp. There would be no more boasts from him that day!

The baby sensed the familiar smell of his mother and felt the warmth of her body against his. He smiled, and looked lovingly into her eyes. There was no more crying.

'I think the master Glooskap has learned an important lesson today, Wasis,' she said.

'Goo!' said Wasis, and they both went back inside.

And that is how the greatest of gods was defeated by the smallest of children and why whenever a baby says 'Goo!' it is to remind us of the time when Wasis put Glooskap firmly in his place.

BLACK BIRD, BRIGHT SKIES

Today, the land of the Canadian Inuit has daylight for half the year and night for the other half. But, according to an Inuit myth, that wasn't always so. It used to be a place of eternal night.

Once, back in the mists of time, the home of the Inuit was a place of total darkness. It was a bleak place of frozen wastes, where the biting cold cut right through the furs worn by the Inuit and sank its teeth into the very marrow of their bones. But worse than the cold was the never-ending night. Midnight or midday, the sky was as black as the shapes of the seals swimming beneath the ice.

In this darkness, babies were born, igloos were built and animals were hunted. Time seemed meaningless, because there were no days to count. The people of this terrible wasteland had only their seal-oil lamps to lighten their darkness.

To pass the time, the Inuit spent much of their lives indoors telling each other stories, but one of the most popular storytellers wasn't a human at all. He was a crow.

Unlike the Inuit, this bird had travelled far and wide. In one hour, his wings could carry him further than it took a man or woman to walk in a day on the treacherous ice with no sunlight to guide them. But, then again, hours and days meant nothing to the Canadian Inuit.

The crow told them of all the other lands he'd seen and of a thing called daylight.

'What is this daylight you speak of?' asked a young hunter. 'I do not understand.'

'It is brighter than the lightning that lights up the sky in a storm,' said the crow. 'But, unlike lightning, it isn't gone in a flash.'

'You mean the sky stays bright?' said the young hunter.

'Yes.' said the crow. 'Instead of the sky being as dark as the pupils in the centre of your eyes, it is as light as the white that surrounds them.'

'How can this be possible?' asked an old woman. 'I have lived longer than any of you sitting in this circle, and I have never seen this thing you call daylight.'

'None of us has really seen *anything* clearly!' cried the young hunter. 'We live in a world of shadows… a world lit by the yellow glow of our seal-oil lamps. Without that, we would be completely blind.'

'Then bring us some of this daylight, Crow, to help us in our daily lives,' pleaded the old woman. 'Not to prove the truth of what you say, for we do not doubt your word, but to help us,' she said.

Crow was always eager to help the Inuit. He had no real reason to visit their land, but they were his friends and that was why he always returned to them.

'Yes,' added the young hunter. 'Will you travel to the world of daylight and bring back a piece for us?'

'I'll try,' said the crow.

The next morning – though no one could tell that it was morning, for the sky was still black – the crow set off on his journey. A crowd of people had gathered in the darkness to see him off. 'Good luck,' they cried, but the moment he took to the skies they could no longer see their friend, for his feathers were as black as the air on which they flew.

On he flew until he saw a glimmering of light on the horizon. At last, he had reached the land of daylight and then – and only then – did he settle down, completely exhausted, to sleep.

When the crow awoke, he thought of the task that lay ahead of him. The Inuit were good people. Because food was scarce in their land, they were always happy to share what little they had between them. Crow knew that this wasn't the way of all people. He knew that those who owned daylight would not willingly give him a piece as a gift, however small. He would have to steal it.

Crow flew to a village and looked for the house of the chief, because he knew that the most important person in the village would be in charge of daylight. He rested on the window ledge and saw a small boy crawling around on a bearskin rug, watched by his loving grandfather, the chief.

Crow could see from the chief's expression that he loved his grandson dearly and that he'd do anything for him. The boy could ask for anything and, to make him happy, his grandfather would give it to him – Crow had no doubt about that.

Some say that the crow turned himself into a speck of dust and crawled right inside the little boy's ear. Others say that Crow spoke to the boy once the chief had left his house to help his daughter carry in a seal-skin bucket of water. Either way, Crow whispered to the boy: 'Ask your grandfather for a piece of daylight... a small piece will do, with a length of string to hold it by.'

So the excited boy cried, 'Grandpa! Grandpa! Let me play with a small piece of daylight.'

But daylight was far too precious to be played with, so the chief tried to distract his grandson. 'Not now, child,' he said. 'Let me tell you the story of Nanook, the white bear.'

He took down a tiny bear carved from the tusk of a walrus, and put it on a rug next to the boy. Then he began to tell his grandson his favourite story – the Inuit tale of how a polar bear saved a man's life by warming him with his body and catching fish for him to eat, and how he taught the man that bears and humans were brothers.

But, for once, the story did not weave its magic. The boy could think of nothing but the daylight. It was a piece of daylight that he wanted to play with and, after he started crying, it was a piece of daylight he was given – with a length of string to dangle it from.

'Thank you, grandpa,' the boy smiled, holding up the glowing orb.

Before anyone knew what was happening, Crow flapped down from the roof where he had been hiding and snatched the length of string.

He then flew straight out of the door which had just been opened by the boy's father, returning home from a hunt.

Up into the air Crow flew, dodging the stream of arrows that were fired up at him by the chief and his villagers. With him he carried the piece of daylight, glowing like an orange ball. On he flew, never daring to stop as he brought daylight to his friends, the Inuit.

It was only a small piece, of course, because Crow wouldn't have been able to carry anything much larger, but it was big enough to bring his friends light and warmth for half of every year. For the first time, they had natural light to see by. The old woman, the young hunter and all the other Inuit were very grateful for what the crow had done, risking his life to bring them daylight.

'Thank you,' they said. 'We shall never forget what you did for us. Your deeds will be told in stories by our children and their children. Your name will live on amongst our people forever more.'

In a land where hunting is still hard and food is still scarce, the Canadian Inuit never kill crows. They are friends of the birds, and now you know why.

THE CURSE OF THE SNAKE'S MEAT

A Sioux chief and his braves were heading homeward
across the plains. Tired and hungry, they were in search
of food. The chief put his ear to the ground and could
hear what seemed to be the thundering of hoofs...

'Buffalo!' he announced. 'Many buffalo.' His braves were delighted.
They waited – arrows at the ready – to pick off some of the
animals as they passed. Soon the noise grew loud enough for all of
them to hear, and the ground shuddered underfoot.

'There must be a whole herd of them!' said one of the braves with
glee. 'We'll return home with fine hides as well as full stomachs.'

But their excitement soon turned to horror when they saw what
was coming towards them. This was no herd of buffalo – it was a giant
rattlesnake, taller than a tepee. What they thought was hoofs turned out
to be the shaking of the monstrous rattle at the tip of its tail!

Rooted to the spot with fear, the chief somehow managed to pull
an arrow from his quiver and let it loose at this terrifying beast. His aim
was true and the snake was killed with this single, well-placed shot.

Soon, they were all eating snake meat – all, that is, except for the
youngest brave...

That night the braves woke up in screaming terror, to find that
they had no arms or legs and that their skin was turning into scales.
Only the youngest brave remained human, as his friends turned
into wriggling snakes before his very eyes! Saddened and shaken,
he returned to his village and told his tribe what had happened.

In the summer, the snakes came to visit their old village. They did no
harm and slithered across their loved ones who recognized them and so
did not fear them. When winter came, the snakes left and the villagers
discovered that the braves' horses and possessions had gone too.

THE GIANT OF THE LOGGING CAMPS

According to European settler legends, the greatest lumberjack of them all – some say the very first lumberjack – was a giant man called Paul Bunyan.

Mrs Bunyan knew there was something special about her son Paul as soon as he was born. 'Our boy is going to be something big in this world,' she told her husband proudly, but she probably hadn't guessed quite how big.

By the time he could walk, her son was bigger and stronger than most of the men in town. Everyone knew who Paul Bunyan was and it wasn't long before everyone had their own tale to tell about him.

One morning, the townsfolk were awoken by a huge 'BANG' followed by the shattering of glass – and the sound had come from the Bunyan house. People leapt out of their beds, pulled on their breeches and boots, and dashed over to see if they could help.

'What happened?' called out one, as Paul's father walked out of his front door, the ground covered in broken glass. 'Are you all right?'

'We're all fine, thank you, friends,' Paul's father assured them. 'It's just that young Paul has a slight cold and one of his sneezes blew the glass out of all our windows.' The bleary-eyed townsfolk laughed, and went back home for breakfast.

By the time he was a young man, Paul Bunyan wasn't just big – he was huge! No one ever got to measure just how tall he was, because there was no tape-measure long enough. Paul quickly outgrew his home town and decided to become a lumberjack in the forests. The job of the lumberjacks was to cut down trees for wood, so that others could build new homes and the furniture for those homes.

Wood was used to make wagons to carry people and goods, and to make sleepers for the tracks that carried the mighty steam trains.

It was used to build churches, hotels and jails and to make telegraph poles so that people could send messages to each other.

Working as a lumberjack on a logging camp was hard work – *hungry* work – for strong men, and the logging camp Paul Bunyan set up wasn't like any other. Behind it was a lake, but this was no ordinary lake. Instead of crystal-clear, blue waters, this lake was filled with a thick, green, bubbling liquid. This was a pea soup lake – hot and ready to serve, night or day.

And you should have seen the griddle on top of the stove that the lumberjacks used to cook their pancakes. In order to grease it, two cooks had to strap hams to their feet and skate around on them, sizzling in the heat – that's how big it was!

Paul Bunyan's logging camp was the biggest and best there ever was. He did so much business that the book-keeper – who kept a record of all the wood they sold – used more than twenty barrels of ink a week.

'The money we spend on all that ink could be better spent on new axes or extra food for the men,' said the book-keeper. 'Any ideas on how we could make a saving?' he asked Paul Bunyan one day.

'By not dotting your 'i's and not crossing your 't's,' said Paul.

So that's exactly what the book-keeper did and he managed to save six barrels of ink in just over two weeks!

✸

Everything about Paul Bunyan was larger than life – even his pet. This was a great big ox and no ordinary ox at that. This was a giant of an ox and, what's more, it was bright blue. And what did Bunyan call this enormous beast with its sharp horns and huge muscles? Babe.

Babe used to have a whole barn to himself – because he was so big – but he even grew too big for that. One morning, Paul found Babe wearing the barn on his back like a saddle. The ox had outgrown it in the night and now it was stuck on top of him!

There are many tall tales about the adventures of Paul Bunyan and Babe, each more unbelievable than the last. Take the time Bunyan had trouble getting a batch of logs down a winding road to the river.

Logs are straight and corners are bent, and the two don't go well together. There was only one road down to the river, and this winding one was it. Once the logs were in the water, they would be carried down to the sawmill by the current... but Bunyan had to get them down the road first.

He came up with a plan, using his brains and Babe's brawn. He built the ox a harness and tied it to one end of the winding road. With the promise of sugar lumps, Babe pulled the road until all the kinks, corners and winding parts were pulled out of it and it was as straight as a rope in a tug-of-war match.

But it wasn't just straight roads Paul Bunyan left behind him. Some claim he even created the Grand Canyon... by mistake! The canyon is a crack in the earth in Arizona that's over two hundred miles long and more than a mile deep in places. The story goes that it was made by Bunyan's enormous pickaxe as he dragged it behind him on the ground – and he didn't even know he was doing it.

It seems that Paul Bunyan really did help to shape North America – in more ways than one!

THE MAN WHO PLANTED TREES

For the early European settlers who travelled by wagon to the unknown west, apple trees provided shelter, food and a taste of home. Legend has it that most of the trees were planted by John Chapman, remembered to this day as Johnny Appleseed.

Johnny Appleseed was happy where he was. He'd heard stories of the west – a wild place of endless plains, huge mountains and thick pine forests – and could think of no good reason why he should leave the safety of his beloved Massachusetts apple farm.

Johnny's farm was acre after acre of orchard, with hundreds of apple trees that bore beautiful blossom in the spring time and delicious apples in the summer. Johnny loved his farm.

Like those around him, Johnny Appleseed was a simple, God-fearing person. He worked six days a week and went to church on the seventh. He was happy with life and happy to be in a country where there was enough land to share.

He loved the people, the language and the food. And the food he loved most of all was apple pie, made from the apples from his very own farm. That Johnny's favourite food was apple pie came as no surprise to anyone. What did come as a surprise was his announcement one day that he himself was heading west.

'But why are you leaving?' asked a friend when he heard the news.

'Because an angel asked me to,' said Johnny. 'He came right out from behind a bush and gave me a mission in life.'

'You?' his friend said, smiling in surprise. 'Why you of all people, Johnny? All you know about is apples!'

'Which is why I was chosen,' said Johnny. 'My mission is to walk west, planting apple seeds as I go.'

And that's exactly what he did. He rode no horse or mule. He carried no gun – just a few supplies, his precious apple seeds and a spade to dig the soil over with – which is how he got the name Johnny Appleseed.

Johnny Appleseed planted more than just apple seeds on his incredible trek westward. He planted plenty of goodwill too. He cared about animals as well as people. One time, he spent a cold winter's night sleeping out in the snow rather than force a mother bear and her cubs out of a warm, hollow log that would have made an ideal shelter for him.

Wherever he went, he was made welcome. By the time he was an old man, he'd planted apple trees right across the plains. Some say that if it wasn't for Johnny Appleseed, there wouldn't be the phrase 'as American as apple pie'!

Then one day the angel appeared to Johnny a second time. 'Your work here is done,' he told the old man. 'Come plant a few apple seeds in heaven.'

So Johnny and the angel left the earth together, leaving behind a country filled with beautiful orchards full of tasty apples.

KING OF THE WILD FRONTIER

Davy Crockett was a real-life American hero
who died in the Battle of the Alamo of 1836.
But there are some stories about this legendary
man that are a little hard to believe...

One day, Davy Crockett and his friend Mike were out hunting.
'I've found a new way to catch racoons,' Davy told Mike.

'How's that?' asked Mike, eager to learn a new trick.

'What's the first thing that happens when a racoon hears you coming?' asked Davy.

'He runs up a tree,' said Mike.

'Then what does the little fellow do?' asked Davy.

'He watches you,' said Mike.

'And while he's watching me, I grin right back at him,' said Davy.

'And?' asked Mike.

'And,' said Davy Crockett. 'I'm so ugly that he falls right out of his tree when he sees me!'

Mike roared with laughter. 'Even you ain't that ugly, Davy!' he said.

'Shh!' whispered Davy. 'See that racoon up there?'

Mike peered into the gloom. 'I can't say I do,' he replied.

'There,' said Davy. 'You can just see its eye peering out at us through the pine needles at the top of that fir tree.'

'If you say so,' said Mike.

So Davy Crockett stood up and stared right into the racoon's eye. He gave it one of his ugliest grins... and the bark fell off the tree!

Mike dashed forward. 'That was no racoon's eye,' he gasped. 'That was a knot in the wood. You grinned such an ugly grin that you frightened the bark right off the tree!'

Just then, a real racoon ran into the clearing.

It froze in its tracks as it caught sight of the two hunters and peered up at Davy. 'You're Mr Crockett – the finest hunter these woods have ever known,' it said.

'That's true,' said Davy, proudly. 'I killed 105 bears in under a year.'

'Then it would be an honour to be shot by you, Mr Crockett,' said the creature. 'Please fire away.'

Davy was deeply moved. 'After what you said, I'd sooner be shot myself than shoot you,' he sniffed, a tear forming in his eye.

'Why thank you,' said the racoon, hurrying off into the wood. 'It's not that I doubt your word,' he called back, 'but I think I'll be off before you change your mind.' With a flash of his tail, he was gone.

Davy looked at Mike. Mike looked at Davy.

'Do you think we've just been tricked by an animal?' asked Mike.

Davy Crockett shrugged. 'One thing's for sure,' he said. 'That was the cleverest racoon I've ever met!'

He may have been outsmarted by a racoon, but Davy Crockett was also a hero. When Halley's comet came speeding towards Earth in 1835, some say that he snatched it by its fiery tail and sent it spinning harmlessly into space.

MAMA AND THE HAIRY MAN

There are a number of different African-American folk tales about the Hairy Man in the forest. He wasn't so much a fierce monster as a troublesome one, but he could be tricked...

When Wiley went out walking, he usually took his two dogs with him, because his mama was worried that the Hairy Man would get him. 'He got your father and now he wants you!' she warned him.

One day, Wiley was in the forest about to cut down some wood, when a wild pig went squealing by. Before Wiley had a chance to stop them, both his dogs chased off after it... and who should appear in the clearing? Why, the Hairy Man, of course.

Even though Wiley had never laid eyes on him before, he had no doubt who it was. The Hairy Man was very tall, very hairy and had great big teeth. He was the ugliest, hairiest, tallest man Wiley had ever seen but – come to think of it – the Hairy Man wasn't really a man at all. He was a monster... and this monster was grinning straight at Wiley.

Wiley ran up the nearest tree. He knew that the Hairy Man couldn't follow him, because he'd seen his feet. The Hairy Man's feet were like cow's hoofs and Wiley knew that cows can't climb trees!

'Come on down, Wiley,' said the Hairy Man, 'and I'll show you some powerful magic!'

But Wiley wasn't going to fall for that trick. 'My mama knows all the magic I'll ever need,' he said, which was true. Mama was a root doctor. She knew the magic of the old African ways. 'If I come down there, all you'll do is put me in that big sack of yours,' said Wiley, staying put.

So the Hairy Man grabbed Wiley's axe and began chopping away at the trunk of the tree. It wouldn't be long before the tree came tumbling down with Wiley in it.

'Wait, Hairy Man!' he called. 'It's time for me to do some praying.'

'If you must,' said the Hairy Man, who didn't really understand these things. He stopped chopping.

Instead of praying, Wiley called out 'Hoooo-Eeeeee!' but, because Hairy Man wouldn't recognize a Christian prayer if you shouted one into his ear, he didn't realize he'd been tricked... until Wiley's hounds came running towards him through the forest. The Hairy Man ran off between the trees.

The next time Wiley met the Hairy Man his dogs were tied up back at home, but he remembered a new trick his mama had taught him.

'Good afternoon, Mister Hairy Man,' he said politely. 'Mama tells me that your magic is really strong. She says that you can turn yourself into any kind of animal.'

'Your mama's right,' said the Hairy Man. 'I can turn myself into an alligator or a giraffe or a –'

'Oh,' said Wiley, looking disappointed. 'Mama says turning into those kinds of creatures is easy. I was thinking you'd try something really difficult like a possum.'

'Difficult?' laughed the Hairy Man. 'I can turn into a possum as easy as that!' and he turned himself into a possum.

Before the possum had time to know what was happening, Wiley had rolled him into his own sack and tied a knot in the top – just as his mama had told him to. But then the bag went flat, and an ant crawled out of a tiny hole in the top. Wiley was up the nearest tree in a flash.

'It was clever turning into an ant like that,' said the boy, 'but can you make things disappear?'

'Like what?' asked the Hairy Man.

'Like rope,' said the boy.

'It's done,' said the Hairy Man.

'You mean you've made all the rope for miles around disappear?' asked Wiley.

The Hairy Man nodded. 'Including the rope that was tying up my dogs?' grinned Wiley, then shouted, 'Hoooo-Eeeeee!'

Muttering to himself, the Hairy Man hurried off into the forest. Wiley hurried home to tell Mama what had happened.

Mama decided that it was time to sort out this Hairy Man once and for all. She knew that if you could trick a monster like him three times, he'd have to leave you alone. That was the way of things. She made some careful preparations, then used her powers to summon the Hairy Man to her home.

'I've come for Wiley,' said the Hairy Man. 'If you don't let me have him, I'm going to make your hens stop laying, your cow's milk dry up and your goat go lame. What do you say to that, Mama?'

'Are you saying that if I give you my baby, you'll leave the rest of us alone forever?' she asked.

The Hairy Man nodded his big, hairy head. 'Yes,' he said.

'You promise?' asked Mama. 'Because you know there's no going back on your word.'

'Promise,' said the Hairy Man, jumping up and down excitedly.

'Then take my baby,' said Mama. 'He's asleep in his bed.'

The Hairy Man ran over to the bed, pulled back the sheets and snatched up the baby that was lying there.

But this wasn't Mama's baby boy, Wiley. This baby wasn't even human. What the Hairy Man held in his hands was a squealing pig.

'This isn't your baby!' cried the Hairy Man.

'Oh yes it is, Hairy Man,' said Mama. 'I own his mother, the sow, and I owned him too – only he's yours now!'

Wiley came out of hiding with his two dogs. 'That's the third time we've tricked you, Hairy Man,' he laughed. 'So you'll have to leave us alone. We've won!'

Defeated, the Hairy Man went sulking back to the forest, where he's probably still muttering to himself to this day.

BRER RABBIT AND THE TAR BABY

The Brer Rabbit stories were first told by African-American slaves, and grew out of animal myths from the African homeland. 'Brer' means brother. These stories were first written down by a journalist from a European background, called Joel Chandler Harris.

'Rise and shine, Brother Fox!' said Brother Rabbit one bright morning, strolling past his sleepy-eyed enemy. Now, Brother Fox was bigger than the rabbit, stronger than the rabbit and had sharper teeth than the rabbit, but Brother Rabbit was always getting the better of him!

Brother Fox planned to change all that – forever. The reason why he looked so bleary-eyed and half-asleep wasn't because that noisy Brother Rabbit had just woken him. No, the reason why Brother Fox was tired was because he'd been up to mischief in the moonlight.

He'd crept to the tar pit, where the black pitch bubbled out of the ground, and had shaped some tar to look like a baby rabbit.

Fox then took the tar baby and sat it in the middle of the dirt track that he knew Brother Rabbit took to his lettuce patch every morning. Then he crept back home and curled up, pretending that he'd been asleep there all night.

When the rabbit reached the tar baby, he greeted it. 'Good morning, youngster,' he said. 'Where's your mama and papa?'

Not surprisingly, the tar baby said nothing, because that's all it was: a baby made of tar. So Brother Rabbit gave it a good shake – only to find that his paws stuck to it like glue. He then used his back legs to try to pull himself free from the sticky tar, and they got stuck too.

Then Brother Fox popped up. He'd been hiding in a ditch, watching all the time. 'It looks like I'll be having rabbit stew tonight!' he laughed.

'I think I'm going to cook you on the fire!' he said, grabbing Brother Rabbit by the ears.

'Oh that's all right then,' said the rabbit. 'I thought you were going to throw me into the prickly patch of briars over there.'

'On second thoughts, I'm going to skin you, then eat you,' said the fox, annoyed that the rabbit didn't seem frightened by his threat.

'Just so long as you don't throw me into the briar patch,' Brother Rabbit pleaded.

'Or I could hang you from a tree,' said Brother Fox.

'Sounds nasty,' agreed Brother Rabbit. 'But not as nasty as the briar patch.'

'Then it's into the briar patch you'll go!' cried the fox. Pulling the rabbit free of the tar baby, he threw him up in the air... and Brother Rabbit landed in the prickly briar patch.

'Thank you for letting me go, Brother Fox!' Brother Rabbit shouted. 'You're forgetting that us rabbits were born and raised in the briar patch!' and, with that, he hopped away.

Just as a slave can trick his master with cunning, once again Brother Rabbit had got the better of Brother Fox.

WHEN PEOPLE HAD WINGS

Myths of flying people, such as this one, were borne out of slavery. Africans were kidnapped, brought to North America against their will and forced to work as slaves, often for cruel masters. This myth is a story of hope and freedom.

John awoke with the sunrise. There was no breakfast for him, just more hard work in the cotton fields. His legs were sore from the Driver's whip and his belly ached with hunger. But still he worked all morning alongside the others, picking cotton under the hot sun.

Then the whispering started. There wasn't supposed to be any talking, and the Overseer rode his horse between the cotton pickers, making sure that everyone was working hard. So the news – the joyous news – was whispered from person to person that Master Tom's slaves on the other side of the hill had sprouted wings and flown away.

'What do you mean flown?' whispered John to the old man who was doing the telling.

'What I say,' said the man. 'Didn't anyone ever tell you that back in Africa people can fly?'

'My papa's from Africa, but he can't fly,' John protested, still picking cotton in case he caught the cruel eye of the Overseer.

'That's because we lost the power when we were brought across the ocean,' said the old man. 'Our wings just shrivelled up and died.'

'It's true,' whispered Mary. 'I used to have wings – blacker than the blackbird's, glinting in the sun. But I lost them – the power and the wings.' She suddenly looked sadder than she'd ever looked before, as she remembered long-lost days of soaring through the African skies.

'Then why do Master Tom's slaves still have the power?' whispered John. 'And why didn't they fly away before now?'

But there the conversation stopped, because the Driver strode past with his whip, glaring at each of them in turn.

When he had passed, the old man answered John: 'Because the power was given back to them by the One Who Remembers – a seer with the gift to say the words that cause wings to grow,' he said.

'Why didn't he share the words?' asked John. 'Then someone from Master Tom's plantation could have told us!'

'Once the words are spoken and the magic has acted, they're forgotten by all except the one who spoke them,' sighed Mary. 'That is the way with some African magic.'

John had a heavy heart. 'If only the One Who Remembers was in our field,' said John.

'But I am,' said the old man, and he spoke the secret words.

Then he stood in the middle of the field and cried: 'Join hands!' and all the slaves hurried forward and linked hands.

'Back to work!' cried the Overseer, galloping towards them.

'Fly!' said the old man, and John felt his shirt tear as his newly-grown wings ripped through the cloth, and he and everyone else in the circle took to the air.

They were flying! They were free!

COYOTE AND THE STORY OF DEATH

Most Native North American tribes tell tales of the fight between good and bad gods. Coyote appears as a bad god in many different tribes' myths. This is the story of how he brought death to humans, then regretted it.

When the world began, there was only water, or so the Maidu say. There was no land, no plants, no animals and no people – just water, with the gods Kodoyanpe and Coyote floating on the surface. The gods decided to create the land and everything on it. Then they created people... but over time there were too many of them.

Kodoyanpe turned to Coyote. 'What shall we do?' he asked. 'There are too many people to fit on the Earth we have created. Soon they'll run out of space.'

'We could stop them having any more children,' Coyote suggested. He didn't care for humans in the way that Kodoyanpe did.

'No, that would be wrong,' said Kodoyanpe. 'Children bring joy and happiness to the tribes and hope for the future.'

'What about death?' suggested Coyote.

'You mean that humans should die in the same way that plants and animals die?' asked Kodoyanpe. 'It seems very cruel.'

'It would solve the problem of there being too many of them,' Coyote said. He really didn't care.

'But that would make everyone so unhappy,' Kodoyanpe protested. 'They would miss their loved ones terribly.'

'They'd get used to it,' snapped Coyote. Because Kodoyanpe seemed so concerned about these people, Coyote was beginning to enjoy having the opposite view. He didn't like it that Kodoyanpe always seemed to get his own way.

'I have an idea,' said Kodoyanpe. 'What if they were to come back to life after a while and change places with the next group whose turn it was to die?' He smiled broadly.

'No,' said Coyote. 'Death should be the end for people. There should be no going back.'

Now, according to a tale the Caddo tribe tell – a tribe that lives far, far away from the Maidu – Coyote was overruled. It was decided that when people die they should stay in a special house built by the chief shaman, until it was time to come back to life and return to their tribe and family. So, when the time was right, the first person – a man – died and his spirit was whisked away on a whirlwind to the shaman's house.

But Coyote would have none of it. Under the cover of darkness, he turned himself into the form of a vicious wild dog, like those we now call coyotes after him. He slunk into the doorway of the house for the resting dead and waited.

When the dead man's spirit reached the house, it found the entrance blocked by this frightening beast and dared not enter. So, instead of resting a while and then returning to life, the dead man's spirit was condemned to search the skies for the path to the land of the spirits. When, at last, it found its way and entered that land, there was no way back... and that's how it has been for everyone since.

But according to the Maidu people, Coyote had his way much more easily. He argued and argued with Kodoyanpe until his brother god finally gave in and accepted the suggestion that humans should not come back to life. Either way, in both stories, Coyote won and death really did mean the end of life for humans.

Kodoyanpe and Coyote went to live amongst the people. Kodoyanpe had always loved the people he'd created and Coyote had never understood that love – until he had a son of his own. Coyote loved that little boy more than he could have imagined possible, so he was overcome with grief when the boy was bitten by a snake.

'I'm dying, father,' said the boy. 'I can feel the poison in my veins. Help me.'

Coyote snatched up the boy and hurried with him to see the chief shaman. 'You must help him,' cried Coyote. 'He has been bitten by a snake.'

The shaman looked at him sadly. 'You are a god and you can do nothing, mighty Coyote!' he said. 'How do you expect me – a mere human – to do what you cannot?'

'But you must try,' said Coyote, thrusting his son into the shaman's arms. 'You are a medicine man.'

The shaman looked down at the still body of the boy. 'I'm sorry, Coyote,' said the shaman. 'There is nothing any of us can do now. Your child is already on his way to the land of the spirits.'

Coyote threw back his head and howled with rage like a wild dog. 'Will no one save my son?' he wailed. Then he went off in search of Kodoyanpe and, when he found him, pleaded with him. 'Kodoyanpe, I was wrong!' he said. 'Death shouldn't be the end. Help me bring my son back to life. I cannot bear to be parted from him.'

Kodoyanpe looked at Coyote and the lifeless boy in his arms. It saddened him that he could do nothing to help, but death meant death and that was of Coyote's own making.

'I'm sorry,' said Kodoyanpe and he truly was, for he hated to see anyone suffer such grief, 'but what's done is done. We cannot undo it. Death is for ever.'

Coyote howled once more. '*Cannot* undo it, or *will not* undo it?' he howled.

His voice became a terrible snarl and his shape changed until he became a wild dog once more.

'Grieve for your son, but do not be angry,' urged Kodoyanpe. 'Remember, it was you who wanted death to be the end!'

With his son dead and haunted by guilt and anger, Coyote roamed the earth in his new form, making mischief wherever he went.

In time, Kodoyanpe lost patience and warned the people against his brother god, Coyote.

'Kill him if you find him,' he ordered. 'For, though the thought of killing him saddens me greatly, as long as Coyote is in the world, we will never be free from evil.'

After many adventures, a group of people chased Coyote on to a tiny island, where no food grew, and surrounded it in their canoes.

'We've trapped him!' said one.

'There's no escaping now,' said another. 'We'll starve him out, so he'll either die of hunger –'

'Or we'll kill him when he tries to escape,' said the first. 'Either way, that'll be an end to all that is bad in the world.'

But Coyote was too clever for them. As evening came he turned himself into a mist and drifted off the island on the breeze. Once clear of them, he let out a great howl of victory, and the people knew that he had escaped from them.

Seeing the people close to despair, Kodoyanpe told them to build a giant canoe – big enough for everyone to fit inside. With everyone on board, Kodoyanpe then flooded the earth, in the hope of drowning Coyote... but Coyote had disguised himself and slipped on board with the others.

As the vast canoe drifted past the peak of a mountain – the only piece of earth not covered by the flood – Coyote leapt on to the mountain, which is how the Maidu people came to call it Canoe Mountain.

'This piece of land belongs to me now,' Coyote declared, turning back into the form of a wild dog.

Kodoyanpe had to admit defeat. There was no way that he could ever rid the world of his cunning brother. This is why Coyote is still out there somewhere, and why we still have evil in the world today.

INDEX

First published in the UK in 1998 by
 Belitha Press Ltd
  London House, Great Eastern Wharf,
  Parkgate Road, London SW11 4NQ

Copyright in this format © Belitha Press 1998
Text copyright © Philip Ardagh 1998
Illustrations copyright © Belitha Press 1998
Philip Ardagh asserts his moral right to
be identified as the author of this work.

ISBN 1 85561 758 7

British Library Cataloguing in Publication Data
for this book is available from the British Library.

Editor: Julie Hill
Designer: Jamie Asher
Educational consultant: Liz Bassant
Series editor: Mary-Jane Wilkins

Printed in Hong Kong